Let's Pretend

Stories by Michael Jeans

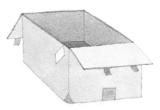

Oxford University Press 1987

Oxford University Press, Walton Street, Oxford, OX2 6DP

Oxford New York Toronto
Delhi Bombay Calcutta Madras Karachi
Petaling Jaya Singapore Hong Kong Tokyo
Nairobi Dar es Salaam Cape Town
Melbourne Auckland

and associated companies in
Beirut Berlin Ibadan Nicosia

Oxford is a trade mark of Oxford University Press

ISBN 0 19 279827 8

Printed in Hong Kong

The Sagging Bridge

A piece of blue material or blue paper for the water.

Get on your hands and knees to be a bridge across the harbour.

Ships would come from all over the world just to sail under this bridge and into the harbour.

One day an octopus tried to come in but the harbour master was cross. 'I don't want a slithery octopus in my harbour!' he said.

The octopus was sad — sad because the harbour master wouldn't let her under the bridge. She only wanted to see what it was like on the other side.

One day the bridge fell asleep. He had had too much to eat for dinner and the sun was hot, so he just couldn't keep awake. As he slept, he sagged.

There wasn't room for the Sea Spray to get under. It was angry. It had come all the way from Yummo-Popo and it couldn't get into the harbour.

The harbour master was in despair. What could he do? He didn't like angry ships shouting at him. Then he heard . . .

. . . a call from out at sea. It was the octopus waving from the waves. 'I'll help you. I know what to do.'

The octopus got under the bridge, raised her tentacles and tickled the bridge. The bridge woke up. It laughed so much it straightened itself out.

The harbour master laughed too. He was so happy. He called to the ship: 'You from Yummo Popo! Why don't you come into the harbour?'

Now whenever a ship enters the harbour, it flies all its flags and the band plays in honour of the octopus — now the Official Bridge Tickler.

The Ostrich and the Beaver

A feather duster or a bunch of brightly coloured material.

Find a way of putting it on so that you have a tail.

Once there was an ostrich. She had the finest ostrich tail in the garden. This was because she was the only ostrich in the garden.

She also had long legs — the longest legs in the garden. She was able to run so fast she sometimes became quite dizzy. But she couldn't fly.

Other birds flew in to eat the food that was put out for them on the bird table. They were safe from the cat there.

They taunted her with stories about their holidays. In winter they flew to Africa and had picnics on the beach. She would have liked that.

Not far away, a beaver was felling a tree. He did this by biting through the wood. He used the trunks he had collected to . . .

. . . build a dam across the river. The water couldn't get past. It rose up and formed a pool in which he had his bath on Fridays.

Today he was fed up with chewing trees. He was looking for something else to bite on, when he saw the bird table.

He started eating. It was quite delicious. It tasted of sausages, kippers, and custard. He carried on chewing away until he had bitten right through it.

Eventually the table collapsed. The food spilled on to the ground. The birds were very upset. They had nowhere to eat their meals.

But the ostrich knew what to do. She put the bird table on her back. She was now the most popular bird in the garden.

The Iceberg Goes on Holiday

A sheet.

Put it on and you can be an iceberg.

The iceberg went off on his summer holiday. He bought his ticket at the station and asked the station master which was the train for the seaside.

Many of the passengers were very surprised to see an iceberg travelling on the train.

When he got to the beach he saw holiday makers playing on the sand and swimming in the sea.

He thought he'd have a swim too. He put on his swimming costume and water wings. Then he jumped into the sea.

The other bathers didn't seem very
pleased to see him. They all rushed out
of the water shivering and very cross.
'Go away', they shouted.

They told him he'd made the water too
cold. He was very sad. So, to cheer
him up, they gave him a present to take
back with him.

When he got home to the snow and ice the whales and the penguins, who had all missed him, were very pleased to see him back.

They all wanted to know whether he'd brought them anything. He said that they must wait and see.

That night by the cold light of the moon, when no-one was looking, he set to work with the present he'd been given.

In the morning all his friends laughed when they saw what he'd made. They had never seen a rabbit before. But now there were snow rabbits everywhere.

Mind that Owl!

The frame of an old pair of spectacles or sunglasses.

Put them on, look very wise, and you're an owl.

This owl is asleep in a tree. Owls fly about at night looking for food. Then they go back to their tree to sleep through the day.

Once there was an owl who always forgot to go back to her tree. She spent the day sleeping in the most unlikely places.

Sometimes she dozed off in the middle of a field. The farmer ploughing the field had to drive his tractor round her.

The farmer didn't like this. When other farmers saw what had happened to the lines in his field, they thought he wasn't very good at ploughing.

The man painting the white line down the middle of the road didn't like it either. He just had to paint round the sleeping owl.

The owl was a nuisance at the race course too. The horses had to jump over her although the race wasn't supposed to have jumps.

It got so bad that the farmer, the white-line painter, and the race horses held a meeting to see what could be done about the owl.

The meeting went on so long that when the people came out of the town hall it was dark. They couldn't see their way home.

Then they heard a 'hoot hoot' and the owl appeared. She had woken up for the night. She led all the race horses safely back to their stables.

Finally she took the white-line painter to his home. His wife was so grateful that she gave the owl a special scarf to keep her warm.

The Great North Pole Theft

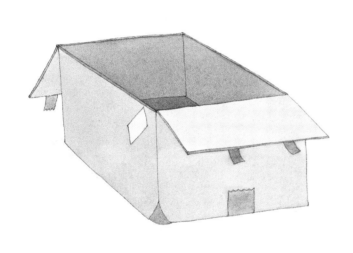

A cardboard box from the supermarket — large enough to sit in.

You could add a broom for the mast and a newspaper sail. You will need some string or sticky tape to stop the broom from falling over.

The boat was bringing Captain Meridian back from a long voyage. He had sailed round Africa and he was looking forward to a cup of tea.

But before he could even tie up his boat, a walrus arrived. He brought with him some dreadful news; someone had taken the North Pole.

He told the captain that there wasn't a moment to lose. 'You must set sail immediately and help us find it', he said.

Captain Meridian said he didn't know where the North Pole should be. 'Don't worry,' said the walrus, 'I'll lead you there.'

When they came to where the North Pole should have been, there was just a hole in the snow. 'We must find it,' thundered the captain.

After weeks of skiing across the snow, Captain Meridian and the walrus found the missing pole.

The polar bears had taken it for their cub sports. The young bears were having a lovely time jumping over it.

The captain and the walrus had an idea. They scooped up the snow to make bricks. Then they built a white and wonderful wall.

The bears were so pleased with their new wall, they let the captain have the first jump over it. The walrus cheered him on.

And so the captain was able to take the North Pole back to where it always should be. After that he sailed home for his cup of tea.